Class 31s

MARK V. PIKE

BRITAIN'S RAILWAYS SERIES, VOLUME 50

Front cover image: This is not quite what it appears to be! 31128 *Charybdis* + 31454 *Heart of Wessex* + 31452 *Minotaur* are seen here at Yeovil Junction sidings in temporary storage. When loco-hauled trains ceased with Wessex Trains during 2006, a rake of coaches (and initially a few locos) were stored here. The locos didn't stay too long but most of the coaches remained here for many years, quite literally rotting away. 4 October 2007.

Title page image: 31128 *Charybdis* heads up the gradient away from Corfe Castle with a train for Swanage. 6 May 2022.

Contents page image: 31454 *Heart of Wessex* + 31452 *Minotaur* are stabled in the bay platform at Salisbury in conjunction with a charter operating on this day. 12 April 2006.

Back cover image: An unusual job for 31190 as it hauls preserved 50035 *Ark Royal* through Salisbury as 0Z50, the 14.20 Eastleigh Works to Derby. The Class 50 had remedial work done at Eastleigh and was heading to Derby for further attention. It has since received a coat of rail blue paint and is based on the Severn Valley Railway in operational condition. 9 April 2015.

Published by Key Books
An imprint of Key Publishing Ltd
PO Box 100
Stamford
Lincs PE9 1XQ

www.keypublishing.com

The right of Mark V. Pike to be identified as the author of this book has been asserted in accordance with the Copyright, Designs and Patents Act 1988 Sections 77 and 78.

Copyright © Mark V. Pike, 2023

ISBN 978 1 80282 671 5

All rights reserved. Reproduction in whole or in part in any form whatsoever or by any means is strictly prohibited without the prior permission of the Publisher.

Typeset by SJmagic DESIGN SERVICES, India.

Contents

Introduction 4
Chapter 1   BR Days – Mid-1980s to 1999 5
Chapter 2   Main Line 2000–Present 23
Chapter 3   Heritage Lines 68
Chapter 4   Open Days and Events 91

Introduction

In the mid-1950s, British Railways commenced a modernisation plan, under which a variety of new diesel locomotive designs would eradicate steam-hauled trains in the UK. Brush Traction at Loughborough was a major player in this plan and, besides developing more powerful locos, also went for smaller designs. British Rail (BR) initially classified its diesels Type 1 to 5 in order of power output and haulage capability and Class 31s, as they later became known, fell into the Type 2 category. Although they were a tad heavy (107 tons), this made them suitable for use on shorter-distance and more lightly loaded passenger and freight trains, and on routes other than main lines. The first examples were put into service on the Eastern Region of BR in the late 1950s. Before long, however, they could be found in use across the country (except north of the border, where they were rare) as the fleet grew in size to reach a total of 263 locomotives.

Within the fleet, a series of subclasses were created over the years, each with a significant number of locomotives. The original twenty 31/0 locos all spent their entire careers allocated to East Anglia but were early withdrawals, with the last few going during 1980. After this, the 31/1s became the 'standard' locos. These were fitted with steam heat boilers and multiple-working compatibility so that they could operate with other types of diesel locomotives as well as with other members of their own class. The fitting of Electric Train Heat (ETH) to several of these in the mid-1970s saw their redesignation as Class 31/4. Much later, towards the end of their careers as a whole, many of these 31/4s were reclassified as 31/5 to reflect the fact that the ETH had been isolated. Later still, the early 2000s saw two locos reclassified again, this time as 31/6. This signified that the ETH could be operated as long as another loco was included within the train; a 31/6 could not operate ETH on its own.

The Class 31 fleet enjoyed sterling service at 12 depots throughout England and, even when BR had dispensed with them, privatisation allowed some of them a whole new lease of life into the 21st Century.

31601 *The Mayor of Casterbridge* **is seen shortly after arrival at Weymouth with a service from Bristol. 3 November 2004.**

Chapter 1

BR Days
Mid-1980s to 1999

With a total of almost 300 examples, the Class 31s could be seen almost anywhere in the country in BR days and were allocated to all regions apart from the Southern and Scottish. That said, they regularly worked on the Southern on both passenger and freight services. The first section of this book portrays locos at work in BR days.

Right: We start this book with a view of the last built member of the class, 31327, moving about the long-lost Bristol Bath Road diesel depot. This loco has since been preserved and can be found on the Strathspey Railway in Scotland. *Circa* 1987.

Below: The former depot at Bristol Bath Road was a very popular place with enthusiasts, being conveniently situated right beside one of the long platforms at Bristol Temple Meads station. A variety of locos could often be seen 'on shed' back in the day. This is 31102, just arriving. *Circa* 1987.

Above: Many of the class were allocated to Western Region depots from the late 1960s right up until their withdrawal in the early 2000s. This is 31425 at Reading with an eastbound parcels train. This loco was scrapped in 1994. *Circa* 1987.

Left: During the 1970s and 1980s, members of the class were regularly seen in South Wales on passenger workings to/from Portsmouth to Cardiff, but they never seemed to be that common on freight trains in this area. This is Railfreight-liveried 31217, passing westbound through Newport with a lengthy oil train and possibly substituting for a larger loco. This particular example was reduced to scrap during 1993. 10 April 1987.

An unusual pairing of 31261+08274 is seen here passing through Doncaster station on an unknown errand, although, as the Class 08 had been withdrawn at the end of 1984, it was probably being taken across to the nearby Works for scrapping. The Class 31 fared a little better, but it too was scrapped in 1990. 5 June 1985.

Now painted in 'Dutch' livery, 31102 is also carrying the name *Cricklewood* and is seen passing light engine through Cardiff Central, probably heading for Canton Depot. The loco was scrapped during 2007. 3 March 1993.

Being quite versatile, members of this class have often been used on charter trains. However, this is the only time any of the class has ever visited the now vanished Weymouth Quay tramway! On a particularly wet day, 31145+31200 are not far from the main BR network as they run light up from the Quay. The charter ran as 1Z40, the 05.40 Preston to Weymouth Quay, and was operated by A1A Charters as 'The Barchester Chronicle'. The two 31s had hauled the train from Stafford. On arrival at the Quay, the train was brought back up the tramway using 33206. The tramway here lasted in limbo for over 25 years until the tracks were removed in the late 2010s. This was an ignominious end to a unique section of line that I feel sure, given the right people in charge, could have been a real money-spinner, especially in the summer months when this seaside town is invaded by holidaymakers. 14 May 1994.

The return charter departed Weymouth main line station at 14.20 and is seen here (still in heavy rain!) passing through Upwey with 31145+31200+33206 all on the front, and all of them on full power on the rising gradient. Upon arrival at Eastleigh, the 31s were removed for fuelling, etc., whilst the 33 took the charter to Salisbury, top and tail with 37274. It then returned to Eastleigh, from where the 31s took the train back to Preston. Of these locos, 31145 was scrapped during 1999; 31200 lasted a while longer until it met the same fate in 2006, and 33206 was cut up during 1997. 14 May 1994.

Towards the end of 1992, a series of popular charters was organised by DC Railtours, involving many types of loco never seen regularly on passenger trains at the time. After arriving from London behind 60029 *Ben Nevis* + 33012, the 09.30 London Waterloo to Paignton 'Solent & Torbay Coaster' then continued forward on its journey behind 31201+31319+33101, seen here waiting to depart from Salisbury. The train was routed direct to Exeter via Gillingham (Dorset) and Yeovil Junction, then and now rarely saw any sort of Class 31 activity. Of these locos, 31201 (once named *Fina Energy*) was scrapped during 2004, 31319 was scrapped during 2007 and 33101 was scrapped in 1997. 29 November 1992.

A hard frost is still very much apparent on a cold morning as we see 31125 stabled between two long-lost diesel multiple-units at Ipswich. This was one of a batch of the class that were built without headcode boxes on the cab roofs, thus gaining them the nickname 'skinheads'! This particular example was scrapped during 2001. 17 January 1986.

The frost has almost gone now as we see 31206 passing through Ipswich with an eastbound engineer's train on the same day as the last shot. This loco was one of the lucky ones and was actually rescued direct from the scrapyard in 2006. It currently resides on the Ecclesbourne Valley Railway. 17 January 1986.

During the mid-to-late 1980s, there was always a steady procession of trains to the West Country, mostly in the summer months. Some of these utilised double-headed 31s, which helped to ease the stretched motive power availability at this busy period. This is the first of a series of shots of these interesting workings. Causing a stir with the 'spotters' at Bristol Temple Meads, 31101+31432 have just arrived with 1V49, the 08.40 Liverpool Lime Street to Paignton service, which the pair had worked from Birmingham New Street. Two rather different outcomes for these locos; 31101 is currently based on the Avon Valley Railway, near Bristol, whilst 31432 was scrapped during 2001. 27 September 1986.

Also at Bristol Temple Meads, this is 31413+31406 with the same train as the previous shot; 1V49, the 08.40 Liverpool Lime Street to Paignton, which this pair had again worked from Birmingham New Street. Note that 31413 has the remains of a white strip amidships, which was probably done by Stratford depot in an attempt to break up the 'boring' Rail Blue livery. 31413 was scrapped during 1997 and 31406 was an early casualty, succumbing during 1991. 9 August 1986.

To show how much of a struggle at times it could be to find locos back in those days, this is solo 31458 waiting to depart from Exeter St Davids with 1M41, the 14.48 Paignton to Liverpool that was normally worked by either a Class 47 or a pair of 31s. Reports at the time implied that the loco put up a great performance! Unfortunately, it was scrapped during 2005. 5 August 1989.

Back to pairs now as we see 31403+31455 arriving at Exeter St Davids with 1V45, the 09.18 Manchester Piccadilly to Paignton, the pair again having worked from Birmingham New Street. Note that 31455 is in the short-lived plain grey Civil Engineers livery. 31403 was scrapped in 2003, whilst 31455 met the same fate in 2000. 5 August 1989.

The second shot from the same viewpoint (and even the same day!), where we see 31426+31425 arriving at Exeter St Davids with 1V46, the 09.33 Stockport to Paignton, having worked from Birmingham New Street once again. In those days you never quite knew what was going to turn up! 31426 was scrapped in 2006, and 31425 in 1994. 5 August 1989.

Above: This time we see 31433+31438 approaching Exeter St Davids with 1V39, the 06.32 Rose Grove to Paignton, which was always a good bet for a pair of 31s. 31433 met its end in 2006, whilst 31438 has been preserved and is currently based on the Epping-Ongar Railway. 30 July 1988.

Left: 31433+31438 viewed in the previous shot are now seen arriving at Exeter St Davids with the return 1M41, the 14.48 Paignton to Liverpool Lime Street, which they would work to Birmingham New Street before giving way to an AC electric loco. 30 July 1988.

On the same day, 31427+31405 arrive at Exeter St Davids with 1V47, the 10.10 Manchester Piccadilly to Paignton. 31427 was scrapped during 2007, whilst 31405 was disposed of during 2000. 30 July 1988.

Above: The last two shots of these holiday trains at Exeter sees 31289+31260 calling with 1V71, the 08.20 Liverpool Lime Street to Paignton service that they had hauled from Birmingham New Street. 3 August 1985.

Right: The same pair powers away from Exeter St Davids on the last leg of their journey. One wonders if the two youngsters enjoying the noise from the front window still have the same enthusiasm for today's modern railway! 31260 was scrapped in 1991, whilst 31289 fortunately still survives in preservation and can be found on the Northampton & Lamport Railway. 3 August 1985.

This time we move north to see 'skinhead' 31107 heading north through Stafford with a short but uniformly 'Dutch'-liveried engineers train, probably heading for Crewe. This loco was later used during a staged collision with a car on a level crossing for an episode of the BBC's *Top Gear* in 2006 and was scrapped in 2009, although it was just about written off in the 'accident'. 22 April 1992.

Shortly after the previous shot, 31166+31178 head south through Stafford light engine. 31166 became very unlucky in its later years as it was preserved and initially worked for a while, but scrapping unfortunately followed in the mid-2010s. 31178, by contrast, was scrapped in 2003. 22 April 1992.

Here we see 31411 arriving at Birmingham New Street, possibly with a service from Norwich. This loco stood out from the crowd at the time, with the addition of a white bodyside stripe and small numbers on the cab side that were probably applied by Stratford depot at some point. It was scrapped during 2005. *Circa* 1987.

In contrasting liveries, 31237+31270 are seen awaiting departure from Stockport, hauling an inspection saloon. It appeared that the 'Dutch'-liveried loco had failed and 31270 was summoned to assist, as it was noted at Crewe earlier in the day (see the next shot). 31237 was scrapped during 2004, but 31270 was another lucky one that can currently be found at Nemesis Rail at Burton-on-Trent, awaiting developments. 7 April 1993.

'Railfreight Coal'-liveried 31270 is captured passing south through Crewe with a short ballast train. The loco was later commandeered to assist the train in the previous shot. 7 April 1993.

Another lucky loco that has since been preserved and has visited a few heritage lines (as we will see later in this book) is 31162. It is seen stabled between duties at Wolverhampton when it was 'just another 31'. It is currently based at the Midland Railway Centre. *Circa* 1987.

Slowly passing through Crewe station is 'Mainline'-liveried 31423 *Jerome K. Jerome,* hauling a couple of similarly painted coaches. Unfortunately, this loco was not so lucky, being scrapped during 2009. 7 April 1993.

The temporary withdrawal during early spring 1993 of the Class 304 EMUs that normally worked services in the North of England led to some Liverpool to Crewe trains being formed of loco-hauled stock and hauled by Class 31s. This is 'skinhead' 31418, just arrived at Crewe with a fresh driver about to take over. The loco is currently undergoing restoration at the Midland Railway Centre. 7 April 1993.

Another loco-hauled substitute arrives at Crewe behind 31438. Some idea of the mix of stock used for these trains can be seen here. This loco was also subsequently preserved and can now be found in working order on the Epping-Ongar Railway. 7 April 1993.

Heading further south, we find 31289+31247 about to pass through Watford Junction with an unidentified southbound freight. 31289 is another lucky one, and can now be found on the Northampton & Lamport Railway but 31247 was scrapped during 2003. 27 February 1990.

On the same day and location as the previous shot, this is 'Departmental Grey' 31457, speeding south with a rake of empty Mk3 stock bound for Wembley. Not too many of the class wore this plain grey colour scheme, and many that did were later modified with the addition of the upper bodyside yellow band, as seen in the following shot. This was quite an early casualty, being scrapped in 1994. 27 February 1990.

Still at Watford Junction but a couple of years later, 31533+31457 pass through the local platforms, also heading south. 31533 was scrapped in July 2006. 22 July 1992.

Moving west, we now see 31276 *Calder Hall Power Station*, just arrived at Westbury to pick up a flask of nuclear waste that had been brought up from Winfrith (Dorset) by a Class 33 or 73 for the continuation of its journey north. The loco was scrapped in 2000, but the nameplates live on, attached to preserved 31130 that we will see later in this book. 19 March 1991.

A new driver boards a smart-looking 31465 at Bristol Temple Meads with a train for Paignton. This loco later went on to do many years' work for Network Rail (NR) on test trains throughout the UK, but has since entered preservation on the Weardale Railway, although it still carries the bright yellow NR livery and is yet to be restored. 29 August 1987.

Reading was another location regularly visited by the class, and this is the first of a few shots from there. Locos could often be seen stabled between duties in the old centre road between platforms 8 and 9, but this has all changed now, following the complete remodelling of the station in the mid-2010s. This is Railfreight-liveried 31116, stabled along with BR blue 47342. The Class 31 was scrapped in 2003, by which time the Class 47 had been scrapped for 11 years, meeting its fate in 1992. *Circa* 1986.

There were many occasions over the years when a Class 31 worked one of the Oxford to London Paddington services, substituting for a Class 47 or 50. This is 31404, arriving at Reading with an unidentified train from Oxford to London Paddington. Note that the loco carries no BR logo and has a steam loco-style shed plate in the headcode box. It was scrapped in 1994. *Circa* 1986.

This time, we see a broadside of a tidy-looking 31466 passing through with an eastbound parcels train. This was one of the last of the class operated by English, Welsh and Scottish Railway (EWS) and the only one to work on the main line in EWS red and gold livery. Possibly due to its uniqueness, it has since been preserved and can be found on the Dean Forest Railway, but at the time of writing was on hire to the Severn Valley Railway. It has also visited other heritage lines, and can be seen in the heritage section of this book. 24 October 1987.

Above: By the very end of the 20th century, most of the class had been withdrawn. 31203 was one of the last in service, and for a few months in early 1999 it was used on crew training/ route learning trips in the Reading area, often doing a round trip as 7Z31 (Old Oak Common to Old Oak Common via Newbury/Trowbridge/Chippenham/ Didcot) using a rake of four-wheeled trucks. The loco is seen pulling up to the signal on the former 'down' through road at Reading with the outward run. 3 March 1999.

Right: 31203 is seen again from a carriage window just west of Reading with the returning 7Z31. Note how many persons are in the cab! 3 March 1999.

One more shot of 31203, this time laying over on the old goods line round the back of Reading station. This was swallowed up during the station rebuilding in the mid-2010s. 3 March 1999.

To conclude this section, we have a couple of images taken at Oxford. This first one is 31425 (with the painted-on name *Hobnob*!), heading south with a short engineer's train, possibly making for Hinksey Sidings about a mile distant. *Circa* 1986.

Although there would no doubt have been many candidates vying for the biggest working of 1988, this one must be somewhere near the top. Railfreight 'red stripe'-liveried 31181 is seen arriving with 1O06, the 07.39 Nottingham to Poole service. Class 31s were very rare west of Basingstoke at this time, and almost unheard of south of Redbridge on the main line to Poole. The loco was deputising for a non-available Class 47, such was the shortage of suitable motive power during the summer service in this era. 27 August 1988.

Chapter 2

Main Line 2000–Present

As mentioned in the last section, most Class 31s had been scrapped by the end of the 20th century but, fortunately, there were many of the class still around in store. Some of these were snapped up by preservationists, whilst others even saw a revival on timetabled passenger trains in the early 2000s. The former South of England-based Train Operating Company (TOC) Wessex Trains operated from 2001 until 2006, regularly hiring locos along with suitable rolling stock for some of their longer-distance and busier services. The Bristol to Weymouth route saw particularly regular use. We start this section with a few of these.

Right: This is 31452 *Minotaur* during a shunt move at Westbury, with InterCity 'Mainline'-liveried 31454 on the other end. In later years, 31452 went on to work with Devon & Cornwall Railways (DCR), but is now privately owned and currently in storage at Great Yarmouth, whilst 31454 is located on the Wensleydale Railway, awaiting restoration. 31 March 2004.

Below: Another shunt move at Westbury, this time with 31602 *Chimaera* and an unidentified loco on the rear. This loco went on to work for Network Rail but was unfortunately scrapped during 2013. 8 October 2003.

In spring 2004, a rake of coaches and 31601 *The Mayor of Casterbridge* were all repainted in Wessex Trains pink livery, and certainly stood out from the crowd! On the very first outing in this bright new livery, it is seen approaching the stop at Castle Cary with 2O86, the 08.28 Bristol Temple Meads to Weymouth service. This loco has since been preserved and can now be found on the Ecclesbourne Valley Railway, though not in this livery, I might add! 27 May 2004.

We are in rural Dorset now as 31459 *Cerberus* is seen approaching Maiden Newton with 2O90, the 14.28 Bristol Temple Meads to Weymouth service. Amazingly managing to avoid those dreaded Beeching cuts of the 1960s, at least for ten years or so until it finally succumbed in 1975, the branch line to Bridport used to pass through a short cutting to the left of the concrete P-way hut in this view. There have been calls to reopen this picturesque branch line over the years but they have all come to nothing so far. The loco has been preserved and can be located on the Nene Valley Railway. 27 July 2002.

Later on the same day as the previous shot, 31190 *Gryphon* is now leading, with the return 17.22 Weymouth to Bristol Temple Meads service approaching Chetnole Halt. After its spell with Fragonset/FM Rail, this loco went on to work with DCR. More recently, it has become another preserved example and is currently to be found on the Plym Valley Railway. 27 July 2002.

After the brief stop at Chetnole, the train is seen pulling away towards Yeovil, with 31459 *Cerberus* bringing up the rear. 27 July 2002.

Yeovil Pen Mill station in Somerset has changed very little since its opening back in 1854. It is quite an unusual set-up, with a rare two-faced platform, and even retains semaphore signalling. This is seen to good effect here as 31468 *Hydra* departs with 2O86, the 08.28 Bristol Temple Meads to Weymouth service. In recent years, this loco was used as a source of spares for other locos and was finally scrapped in 2018. 25 November 2003.

This is 'Mainline'-liveried 31454 *The Heart of Wessex*, passing a nice patch of Rosebay Willowherb on the approach to Dorchester West with 2O86, the 08.28 Bristol Temple Meads to Weymouth service. This loco has since been preserved and is currently on the Wensleydale Railway, awaiting its turn for restoration. 13 August 2005.

On the rear of the train in the previous shot is 31459 *Cerberus*, just about to depart south on the last leg to its destination. 13 August 2005.

Also arriving at Dorchester West but a few months earlier than the last shot is 31601 *The Mayor of Casterbridge* with the same service. The two Class 31/6s were very unusual in that they were through wired for Electric Train Heating (ETH) but could not actually provide it on their own, unlike Class 31/4s. This meant that they could be attached to a train with another loco, and that loco would still able to heat the train via the wiring system installed in the Class 31/6. 30 October 2004.

31601 *The Mayor of Casterbridge* is seen again, this time soon after arrival at Weymouth with a service from Bristol. It is a bit of a shame that no other loco received this livery, as when it was working with the similarly liveried rake of coaches, the train always had an odd loco on one end! 3 November 2004.

Looking rather filthy, 31454 *The Heart of Wessex* is also seen 'on the blocks' at Weymouth after arrival from Bristol. It is interesting to note that at the time, Fragonset were using the well-known 'InterCity' branding on the loco. Although others carried it in earlier years, this loco was the only one treated to InterCity 'Mainline' livery at this time. 26 October 2004.

One of the first visits of the Wessex Trains loco-hauled set to Weymouth was a test run to check clearances and so on. This is 31468 *Hydra* on a very wet and miserable day soon after arriving at Weymouth. 25 November 2003.

Above: Showing off the recently applied InterCity 'Mainline' livery that certainly helped to brighten this gloomy day, 31454 stands at platform 3 at Weymouth, awaiting departure north. Note this was also before it received *The Heart of Wessex* nameplates. 25 November 2003.

Right: A closer look at the livery applied to 31454 at Weymouth and also that wonderful cast crest on the cab side, reminiscent of the ones applied to some of the AC electric locos in their early days on the West Coast Main Line. 25 November 2003.

A little later, 31454 is seen powering away from Weymouth on the start of its journey back to Westbury. The once vast goods yard and carriage sidings used to cover the whole area to the right and behind the train. 25 November 2003.

At the same location as the previous shot, 31452 *Minotaur* starts the assault of the long, rising gradient of around five miles to the summit at Bincombe Tunnel, with the 11.00 Weymouth to Bristol service. 30 June 2004.

Westbury was often an excellent place to view the 31s and stock, as there was often much shunting to be seen. 31454 is heading towards the servicing point in the yard. 13 January 2004.

This is 31602 *Chimaera* at Westbury station with an unidentified service. 12 June 2003.

Heading away from Westbury on the rear of a train heading north is 31454 again. The train is taking the route via Trowbridge, whilst the lines veering off to the right above the first coach lead to Heywood Road Junction, where they join the main line to Newbury and onward to Reading. 29 March 2004.

A little further on from the last shot is Hawkeridge Junction, where the station-avoiding line from the aforementioned main line to Newbury and Reading joins the route to Trowbridge/Bath. This is often used for diversionary purposes at times of engineering work on the Great Western Main Line via Didcot and Swindon. 31128 *Charybdis*, with 31454 on the rear, is passing the junction and approaching Westbury with an unidentified southbound service. As of 2023, 31128 is the only main line-registered member of the class. A more recent shot of it can be seen in the heritage section later in this book. 18 September 2004.

One of the first outings for the loco-hauled set was this one. 31459 *Cerberus* heads away from Salisbury with 1Z80, the 12.41 Southampton to Cardiff Central charter put on for a rugby match at the Millennium Stadium, Cardiff. 9 November 2002.

On the rear of the train in the previous shot, 31602 *Chimaera* heads away from the camera on departure from Salisbury.

Another service regularly worked by 31s was the often very busy Fridays-only 1O98, the 12.00 Cardiff Central to Brighton service. The train is seen here passing Millbrook FLT, headed by 31454. 9 April 2004.

A quick spin round with the camera sees 31128 *Charybdis* bringing up the rear of the train in the previous shot heading through Millbrook (Hants) station. 9 April 2004.

Slowing for the stop at Southampton Central, this is 'skinhead' 31106 *Spalding Town* with the same Fridays-only 1O98, the 12.00 Cardiff Central to Brighton service. After many years working on the main line, this loco has now been preserved on the East Lancs Railway, where it is currently undergoing restoration. 9 October 2004.

Above: This is 31468 *Hydra* just arrived at Southampton Central, again with 1O98, the Fridays-only 12.00 Cardiff Central to Brighton service. 24 October 2003.

Right: On the rear of the train in the last shot is 31454, on what was one of its first outings in InterCity 'Mainline' livery. The resplendent loco is seen bringing up the rear of the train as it departs Southampton Central. 24 October 2003.

Moving away from the use of 31s on timetabled passenger work, we now start a batch of images depicting them working various test trains, the most common trains they operated during the 2000s and occasionally thereafter. This scheme was an early attempt by Railtrack, Network Rail's predecessor, to individualise its locos. Two examples (31190+31601) received it, and 31190 *Gryphon* is seen stabled in the siding alongside Southampton Central station. 26 November 2003.

This location, sometimes referred to as 'The Avenue', has always been a favourite with photographers due to the unusual presence of the huge fir trees either side of the line. When I visited for this shot, the area had been shorn of undergrowth and tidied up, affording this shot (from a public foot crossing) of bright yellow Network Rail-liveried 'skinhead' 31105, heading south with 4Z08, the Bristol Kingsland Road to Derby via Weymouth test train. 19 February 2010.

A further shot of the train was obtained here at Dorchester West as 31105 pulls away on the last leg to Weymouth. This image was obtained by looking over a temporary wall built during the construction of a housing development, a view which I believe is no longer possible. The castle-like building prominent in the background was built as a barracks in the 1880s but closed in the mid-1950s. It is now the Keep Military Museum and worth a visit to anyone with interest in militaria. The loco has since been preserved and can be found in operational condition at the Mangapps Railway. 19 February 2010.

Its days of working regular passenger trains now behind it, this is plain black 31459 *Cerberus*. It is pictured on the pre-electrified Great Western Main Line at South Moreton, just east of Didcot, with 1Z12, the 09.45 Didcot to Didcot via Reading, Basingstoke and Maidenhead test train. This was a very popular photographic location before the overhead wires transformed the area. 28 October 2009.

Quite literally at the end of the day, just as the sun was setting, this is 31459 *Cerberus* again, this time on its return with 1Z12 seen in the previous shot. Note the ever-brightening moon above the train! 28 October 2009.

This incredible sight is certainly not environmentally friendly! The reason for all these fumes is that the two locos, 31190+31106 *Spalding Town*, have just come off Eastleigh Depot after a cold start on a very cold and frosty February morning. The addition of the rising sun behind the fumes has created an almost ethereal image. The locos are unusually working an unidentified test train, comprising just one coach to cover the local area. 7 February 2007.

With 31190 now on the rear, the ensemble was seen again later in the day departing Southampton Central and heading east. Obviously, the smoking issue had still not completely sorted itself out! 7 February 2007.

A couple of examples operated by Network Rail received front end modifications, including a whole host of spotlights for assisting during night duties and tunnel inspections. This is 31285 and its train, stabled at Bristol Temple Meads. When dispensed with by Network Rail, this loco entered preservation on the Weardale Railway. 23 March 2012.

Above: Another loco fitted with the front end modifications was 31233. This became the last operational member of the class with NR in early 2017. It is seen here at North Staffs Junction, just south of Derby, with 1Q04, the 09.52 Derby RTC to Derby RTC (via Reading). This was the last time I photographed a class member on a test train. The loco itself is now preserved and can be found at the Mangapps Railway Museum in an operational condition. 11 February 2016.

Right: Another shot seen on the pre-electrified Great Western Main Line as 31190 approaches Didcot Parkway with an unidentified test train. This view is somewhat different nowadays. 22 November 2007.

31190 is seen again, this time heading south on the approach to Winchester, with a test train heading for Eastleigh Depot. The bridge this shot was taken from has since been rebuilt and it is now very difficult to obtain anything similar to this view, unless you stand on a box or just happen to be around seven feet tall! 7 November 2008.

Revisiting old haunts from its days with Fragonset on passenger trains, 31106, now resplendent in BR blue livery, is approaching Evershot Tunnel on the Yeovil to Dorchester line with 4Z10, the 11.03 Bristol Kingsland Road to Derby RTC (via Weymouth) test train. This is another location that had just been cleared of heavy tree growth, but is marred these days by the addition of a tall radio mast near the rear of the train. 24 September 2009.

Such were the timings of this train that I was able to get another view of 31106 as it headed south near Bradford Peveril, just north of Dorchester. Note the old bullhead rails it is travelling along, still in place at this time. 24 September 2009.

31602, now carrying the name *Driver Dave Green*, was another loco to receive extra headlights, though not as many as 233/285. The loco is seen approaching Yeovil Pen Mill with 3Z14, the 09.16 Bristol Barton Hill to Bristol Barton Hill (via Weymouth) test train. 28 April 2011.

This is the same train approaching Maiden Newton on its return from Weymouth, with the loco now propelling. 28 April 2011.

Above: With some all-too-predictable motive power of the day stabled in the background, 31285 enters the depot complex at Eastleigh with the 3Z07 Hither Green to Eastleigh test train. 23 January 2015.

Left: Back in the British Rail era, seeing any members of the class at this location would have been highly unlikely, except perhaps for an odd railtour at some point. 31106 is seen arriving at London Bridge at the start of a very busy day with 1Q14, the 08.55 Selhurst TRSMD to Selhurst TRSMD. This travelled via London Bridge, Dartford, Gillingham (Kent), Faversham, Ramsgate and Barnham. 26 March 2010.

31106 is seen again, 'on the blocks' after arrival at London Bridge. Of course, since these images were taken, this station has been completely refurbished and remodelled. It is doubtful whether a Class 31 will be ever be seen here again. 26 March 2010.

Above: On the other end of the train in the previous shot is 31602 *Driver Dave Green*, which is seen preparing to depart south out of London Bridge station. 26 March 2010.

Right: Still in the London area, this is 31233 (with 73107 *Spitfire* on the rear) approaching Clapham Junction with 1Q85, the 06.08 Woking Down Yard to Hither Green test train. Once again, back in the early days a member of the class would have been pretty rare at this location. I have a feeling that the 31 was deputising for a non-available Class 73. 12 August 2010.

We are now in Kent as we see 31465 powering through Paddock Wood, propelling the 3Z13 Grove Park to Dollands Moor test train. We saw this loco back in the first section of the book, some 25 years earlier at Bristol Temple Meads. After retirement from Network Rail, it has now found its way into preservation at the Weardale Railway. 20 January 2012.

Above: 31285 is passing through Horley station, about a mile or so east of Gatwick Airport, with an unidentified test train, probably heading for Hither Green Depot. 29 January 2009.

Left: 31285 again, this time propelling an unidentified test train through Fareham on its way south from Eastleigh. 26 March 2009.

A nice bit of late autumn sunshine greets 31106 as it comes around the curve on the approach to Freshford station in the Avon Valley, between Bath and Bradford on Avon, with 3Z14, the 0920 Bristol East to Bristol East (via Weymouth & Swindon) test train. 17 November 2011.

Above: Such are the timings of some of these test trains, especially on the largely single line between Castle Cary and Dorchester Junction, that I was once again able to get ahead of 31106 and grab this shot of its departure from Maiden Newton towards Dorchester West with 3Z14. 17 November 2011.

Right: I decided to stay in the area for the return up from Weymouth. This is 3Z14 again, this time at Stratton, just south of Maiden Newton, now propelling the train north. 17 November 2011.

Still in Dorset, but now on the main Southampton to Weymouth route, we see 31465, passing through Bournemouth station with the 1Q12 Eastleigh to Eastleigh test train. The huge overall roof here was totally refurbished in 2001, after falling into disrepair many years earlier. 3 September 2009.

Another shot of the train in the previous image on its return. 31465 is propelling away from Brockenhurst, in the heart of the New Forest National Park, after a brief signal check. 3 September 2009.

31465 was quite a regular visitor to the area around this time. It is seen here again a few months earlier, this time nearing the summit of the 1-in-50 incline from Parkstone station with 1Q12, the 13.25 Poole Carriage Sidings to Brockenhurst radio survey train. 16 June 2009.

The train later worked back west from Brockenhurst, and then back east again. 31465 is seen here soon after passing Hamworthy on its way towards Poole. The sidings to the left have fallen into disrepair; they were once regularly used as 'overflow sidings' for stabling coaching stock from the many extra trains that ran to the area during the summer months back in the 1950s and 1960s. 16 June 2009.

A very rare location to see a member of the class, even in recent years, is the short freight-only line from Hamworthy to Hamworthy Quay. This, however, is 31233 (with 73107 *Spitfire* on the rear) just arriving with 1Q08, the 09.28 Bournemouth TRSMD to Westbury. This was booked to travel a very circuitous route via Hamworthy and Fratton, then on to Salisbury and its destination. It is amazing to think that out of sight, just to the right of this view, are the remains of the first Poole station that closed to passengers as far back as 1896, with the line being freight only since then! A remarkable survivor. 20 April 2010.

Above: We are now in Surrey, where we see 31106 coming over the level crossing at Wokingham with 1Q14, the 09.22 Clapham Yard to Eastleigh (via many routes in the London suburbs). 4 October 2012.

Left: A further shot of this particular 1Q14 working sees 31106 now on the rear (with 37419 *Carl Haviland* leading) into the large Guildford station complex. 4 October 2012.

With any sort of photography, there is always a certain degree of luck involved, and this very much applies to railways. That is exactly what occurred here as we see 31106 (with 37419 *Carl Haviland* now on the rear again) arriving at Reading off the Guildford line, just as a Paddington-bound HST passes by on the main line, heading towards London Paddington! 4 October 2012.

Above: The Salisbury to Exeter line is quite near my home, and when anything unusual turns up it is always worth a photograph or two! This is 31465 in rural surroundings on the single-line section between Tisbury and Gillingham (Dorset) with the 1Q12 Salisbury to Eastleigh (via Yeovil & Weymouth) test train. 27 August 2009.

Right: Having passed a service train at Gillingham (Dorset), the train in the previous shot is seen climbing to the summit at Buckhorn Weston Tunnel with 1Q12. Since this shot was taken, a huge radio mast has been placed slap bang in the foreground; this and the amount of tree growth makes this view no longer possible. See also page 60. 27 August 2009.

Looking a bit like a model, 31233 approaches Micheldever on the Waterloo to Southampton/Weymouth main line hauling 3Z02, the 10.10 Didcot to Eastleigh test train transit move. This shot was taken through a gap in the trees, almost above the long-abandoned oil storage depot. 16 April 2013.

A few miles further east than the previous picture, we see 31465 (with 31459 *Cerberus* on the rear) passing through Basingstoke with 1Q12, the 09.00 Woking Up Reception to Woking Up Reception test train. In more recent times, trains such as this on third-rail lines usually employ Class 73/9s or, very occasionally, Class 37s. 15 December 2009.

This is 31106 powering north along the single line, just after passing Dorchester West with an unidentified test train that had just visited Weymouth. I have not been back to this spot since, but I believe it is now once again hopelessly overgrown with trees. 27 May 2010.

On to the former Western Region of BR now for the conclusion of this test train sequence. This is 31233, having just passed Fairwood Junction and now approaching Westbury with 1Q10, the 05.12 Westbury to Eastleigh (via Weymouth/Westbury/Salisbury) test train. Unusually, 73107 *Spitfire* was on the other end, so the 31 did most of the work along the way, with the Class 73 acting as a glorified Driving Van Trailer (DVT). 21 April 2010.

Further west, on the approach to Castle Cary, we see a very faded and tired-looking 31105 with 3Q14, the 09.30 Bristol to Didcot (via Weymouth) test train. It is now one of the oldest of the class in preservation at the Mangapps Railway Museum, and is in operational condition. 18 March 2014.

The last test-train shot sees 31106 again entering the fuelling point beside Exeter St Davids station. When one of these trains is in the area for overnight testing, it will often visit this fuelling point in daylight, with a quick trip from the nearby Riverside Yard. In days gone by, Class 31s were no strangers to the West Country, with many working local services from Exeter as well as much further afield. 19 September 2012.

A small batch of charter train images now. This first one shows Fragonset-liveried 31602 *Chimaera* + 31128 *Charybdis* powering away from Southampton Central with an unidentified charter. I think this one was originally advertised as steam-hauled, but hot weather and the risk of fire meant that the 31s were substituted. 11 July 2006.

Just over a week later, another steam loco substitution took place; this time former BR Class 8P 71000 *Duke of Gloucester* was replaced with 31602 *Chimaera* + 31452 *Minotaur*. The pair are seen at Redbridge causeway approaching Totton with 1Z91, the 08.36 Kensington Olympia to Weymouth 'Sunny South Special'. Yes it was actually sunny for a change as well! 20 July 2006.

Another shot of this train sees it having just arrived at Bournemouth. There were once two centre tracks in the station here up until 1967, hence the wide area between the platforms. 20 July 2006.

A few miles further south and we are now at Poole to see 31454+31128 *Charybdis* pass through with 1Z97, the 16.33 Weymouth to London Victoria. Apparently, the whole day was dogged by problems for this particular charter, not least with the original train loco, ex GWR 'King' 6024 *King Edward I* running out of coal by the time it reached Weymouth. This came about due to 31128 failing earlier in the day, necessitating the steam locomotive's having to work further than originally booked. 6024 then had to be hauled from Weymouth by 31454 to Yeovil Junction (where 6024 was originally to have come off the train) for servicing. Later in the day it was decided that it would be too late for 6024 to get back to Weymouth to haul the return charter. It was now getting very late, so rather than go the booked route via Yeovil it was decided that the charter should return more direct via Poole and Bournemouth to try and make up some time, hauled only by the Class 31s. 4 June 2005.

With the dreaded steam ban still in place, this time 31452 *Minotaur* + 31128 *Charybdis* are departing Havant with 1Z92, the 09.30 London Victoria to Chichester charter. This was originally advertised for haulage by 'Black Five' 45231. The large signal box on the left closed in late 2007, but survives to this day due to being Grade 2 listed. 1 August 2006.

To the West Country now for a few charters. This is 31452 *Minotaur* + 31454 *Heart of Wessex* departing Taunton on the last few miles of their journey with 1Z93, the 06.02 Barking to Minehead, and heading for the West Somerset Railway Steam Gala. In this view the huge amount of buddleia bushes to the right of the train wasn't too rampant, but in recent years they have really got out of hand and this sort of shot is much compromised. 7 October 2006.

A most unusual combination this time as 31602 *Chimaera* + 33108 *Vampire* head west through Dawlish Warren with 1Z51, the 04.30 Lancaster to Paignton 'Devonian' operated by Fragonset Charters. Although both were operated by the same TOC at the time, a 31/33 combination anywhere on the network was (and still is) pretty rare. 25 August 2001.

A more standard pairing this time as we see 31602 *Chimaera* + 31601 *Bletchley Park Station X* standing at Newton Abbot with 1Z36, the 08.11 Crewe to Paignton Pathfinder Tours 'Torbay Quarryman' charter. The locos ran round here and headed back east to Exeter St Davids, from where a couple of Class 66s in 'top and tail' mode took the train to Meldon Quarry and then on to Paignton. Here the pair of 31s rejoined and returned the charter to Crewe in the evening. 14 May 2000.

Eleven years later, on a typically gloomy day, 31601 was working for DCR when it was seen with 31190, also by then a DCR loco. They are heading west at Dawlish with a 13-coach 1Z20, the 05.20 Tame Bridge Parkway to Penzance Pathfinder Tours 'Mazey Day Cornishman', which took these two veterans all the way to Penzance. 25 June 2011.

Another unusual combination as 31452 *Minotaur* is seen coupled ahead of ex-BR Standard Class 5 73096 for the relatively short run from Westbury to Cranmore, on the last leg of the journey for 1Z96, the 09.05 London Victoria to Cranmore 'Cathedrals Express' charter. The train had arrived at Westbury from the Reading line with 73096 up front and, although the loco could be turned on the Westbury triangle, it was decided that, to save time, the 31 would be coupled ahead for this short section to Cranmore. There the 31 ran round and led back to Westbury later in the day. 73096 then took the train back from Westbury to London via Salisbury. 6 September 2003.

In the days of loco haulage on London Waterloo to Exeter trains, this bay at Salisbury was often used to stable spare locos. However, one rarely sees a loco here nowadays. 31454 *Heart of Wessex* + 31452 *Minotaur* are stabled in conjunction with a charter operating on this day. 12 April 2006.

Above: To end this section, this series of pictures shows some freight operations in recent years, plus a few other duties performed by the class before most retired from the main line. Apart from Network Rail, DCR have made good use of the class up to the mid-2010s. This is veteran 31190 approaching Banbury with 6Z31, the 10.10 Chaddesden Sidings to Eastleigh Works, with a short rake of wagons for maintenance. 12 March 2013.

Left: A few months later and 31190 was on a similar 6Z32, the 10.42 Chaddesden Sidings to Eastleigh, this time passing Basingstoke with just three trucks. 3 May 2013.

Another regular duty at the time was hauling a Railvac machine (usually during the hours of darkness) that DCR had the contract for in the south. This is 31190 'top and tail' with 31452 (now de-named) for the short journey with 6Z41, the 10.40 Totton Yard to Eastleigh TRSMD transit move passing Millbrook FLT, just west of Southampton Central. 18 October 2013.

Above: 31452 is approaching Basingstoke, this time with a rake of overhauled trucks running as 6Z32, the 11.30 Eastleigh to Bow Depot. 23 October 2013.

Right: Looking almost comical, a couple of trucks are sandwiched between 31452 and 31190 running as 6Z33, the 10.40 Totton Yard to Eastleigh TRSMD. 26 September 2013.

As locos of any description are rare on the Salisbury to Exeter line, as mentioned earlier, it is worth getting them when they do turn up! This mini sequence shows a rare visit of a Railvac to the line, and even rarer shots of it in daylight. Since this date I don't think the Railvac has been back. With both locos wearing DCR green livery, 31601 'top and tail' with 31452 are seen coming down the gradient after exiting Buckhorn Weston Tunnel on the descent to Gillingham (Dorset). 21 September 2014.

Turning quickly around, this is a view of 31452 bringing up the rear of the train. The radio mast mentioned in the middle picture on page 49 is just to the right of shot and the undergrowth that I also mentioned in that shot is now far worse, so much so that you can hardly see the line now! 21 September 2014.

Seen beneath the canopy of a deserted Gillingham (Dorset) station is 31452 on the rear of the same train again, waiting for a service from London Waterloo to Exeter St Davids to cross before departure northward. Note that the old footbridge, made at the long-gone Exmouth Junction Concrete Works during the 1950s, is still in daily use here. 21 September 2014.

The last shot of this mini sequence sees 31601 waiting to leave Gillingham from the down platform. It is interesting to think that 31s have never been common here, and before the privatisation of the railways, a visit from one was just about unheard of. 21 September 2014.

In a view reminiscent of the late 1960s, 31190 is just north of Mortimer on the Basingstoke to Reading line with 5Z31, the 09.23 Eastleigh Works (Arlington) to Crewe LNWR, hauling various items of coaching stock. 12 May 2015.

This is not quite what it appears to be! 31128 *Charybdis* + 31454 *Heart of Wessex* + 31452 *Minotaur* are seen here at Yeovil Junction sidings in temporary storage. When the loco-hauled trains ceased with Wessex Trains during 2006, a rake of coaches (and initially, a few locos) were stored here. The locos didn't stay too long, but most of the coaches remained here for many years, quite literally rotting away. 4 October 2007.

This is the rare sight of 31452 hauling 'Wessex Electric' unit 442405 as 5L46, the 12.30 Eastleigh Works to Ely for storage. I think this is only the second time a Class 31 has hauled a 442, the first being sometime in the late 1980s, when the units were being delivered to Bournemouth Depot. I don't think anyone batted an eyelid back then! 21 October 2016.

The transfer of coaching stock from Barton Hill Depot at Bristol to Wembley was also a contract entrusted to DCR locos, although it did transfer to Direct Rail Services (DRS) in later years. 31601 is hauling an immaculate blue & grey Chiltern Railways Mk3 coach towards Didcot Parkway as 5Z61, the 09.30 Bristol Barton Hill WRD to Wembley LMD. This view is impossible now, for many reasons; the footbridge has been replaced by a caged-in effort, the line has been electrified and the power station in the background has vanished. 12 October 2012.

Just two years later, the cooling towers of the power station had already gone as we see 31452 at a lower elevation, hauling a Chiltern Trains-liveried Mk3 as 5Z34, the 10.13 Bristol Barton Hill WRD to Wembley LMD. Another reason this view has changed drastically is that a huge multistorey car park now dominates the area above the loco. 28 October 2014.

Another year later and things had changed yet again. Just one part of the power station is still extant and 31601, hauling another Chiltern Mk3, has changed livery again, this time into new DCR grey with the name *Devon Diesel Society*. 5Z34, the 10.00 Bristol Barton Hill WRD to Wembley LMD is coming into Didcot Parkway station. 28 September 2015.

An unusual job for 31190 as it hauls preserved 50035 *Ark Royal* through Salisbury as 0Z50, the 14.20 Eastleigh Works to Derby. The Class 50 had had remedial work done at Eastleigh and was heading to Derby for further attention. It has since received a coat of rail blue paint and is based on the Severn Valley Railway in operational condition. 9 April 2015.

To conclude this section of the book, we turn to a few light engine movements. This is 31105 arriving at Weymouth with an unidentified route-learning trip. 19 September 2008.

Another route learner as 31128 *Charybdis* pulls up to the signal at Gillingham (Dorset), heading for Weymouth once again via Yeovil Junction/Pen Mill and Dorchester West. Although there was a small covering of snow on the ground at this time of the morning, it was not as bad as it looked, and the day turned out to be rather pleasant. 1 March 2005.

After spending the night in sidings at Weymouth, 31128 *Charybdis* is pulling into the station ready to work back north. The large signal box to the right was built in 1957 but only lasted 30 years; it was taken out of use in 1987 and was not finally demolished until the 2010s. 2 March 2005.

One last shot of 31128 *Charybdis* as it passes east through Wareham station. This was another location where members of the class were largely unknown in BR days. 2 March 2005.

Prior to gaining BR green livery, 31190 *Gryphon* was in West Coast Railways maroon colours, possibly the only 31 in this livery. It certainly looks rather smart on the loco, sat here in the winter sunshine at Westbury. 8 February 2006.

The last picture in this section shows 31452 on what was its final main line run as 0Z31, the 10.00 Derby to Okehampton/Meldon. The loco worked on the heritage line at Okehampton for a while but has since been moved to private sidings at Great Yarmouth, as the heritage operations at Okehampton were curtailed when NR restored the line for regular passenger train use in the late 2010s. This was to be the last working of a Class 31 on the main line, but 31128 *Charybdis* has since regularly operated on the national network to Whitby. 27 November 2017.

Chapter 3
Heritage Lines

Many examples of the class have worked on the various heritage lines around the UK and seem at home in this situation, being suited to most. This section shows a few that are either resident or have visited some of these lines, mainly in the South of England.

Left: We start with the Avon Valley Railway between Bath and Bristol, part of the old Midland Railway line that ran from Bath to the North of England. The line is now home to two 31s, 31101 and 31130 *Calder Hall Power Station*. Both times I have visited, 31130 has been in action, as witnessed by this first series of pictures. My first visit here was on a damp day in autumn 2012, when the loco was resplendent in the Railfreight Coal livery that it previously carried in the 1990s. It is seen here nearing Oldland Common station, the northern limit of the line. 26 October 2012.

Below: The southern limit of the line crosses a couple of substantial bridges before arriving at Avon Riverside. Here 31130 is slowly crossing what is really a small viaduct, which serves as flood arches for the nearby River Avon. 26 October 2012.

The other bridge is a substantial metal structure that actually crosses the River Avon. This time, 31130 is seen pulling away from Avon Riverside and heading north towards the headquarters of the line at Bitton, which is located roughly midway between here and Oldland Common. 26 October 2012.

Along the whole distance of the line (around three miles), it is accompanied by the Bristol & Bath Railway Path, a nice easy walk (or ride) that is highly recommended. As this was originally a double-tracked main line, there is ample room to accommodate both the railway and the path, as can be appreciated here with the loco coming up the straight section between Avon Riverside and Bitton alongside a well-timed cyclist! 26 October 2012.

Despite the annoyingly persistent drizzle, the loco still looks very smart here at Bitton as it waits to head off to Oldland Common. 26 October 2012.

Another view at Bitton, with the loco waiting to head north. 31130 actually arrived on the line during 2012 and this was one of its first outings. The name carried by the loco was originally bestowed on 31276 during 1988, but for some reason it was transferred to 31130 in 1992. 26 October 2012.

My next visit to the line was seven years later, by which time 31130 had received the original Railfreight livery that it had also carried from the late 80s before donning the livery seen in the previous shots. This first view sees the immaculate loco at Avon Riverside having just arrived from Bitton. 28 September 2019.

Crossing the bridge seen at the bottom of page 68, the loco is now heading north from Avon Riverside towards Bitton. 28 September 2019.

Above: Not long after departing Bitton, the loco comes under the Cherry Garden Lane road bridge as it makes for Oldland Common. 28 September 2019.

Left: The final shot from the Avon Valley. Although it was dry this time, it was very cloudy almost all day, apart from here when I took this shot at Bitton station. The loco is waiting to head south again to Avon Riverside. 28 September 2019.

We now move further south to the Swanage Railway, where the annual diesel gala often attracts a member of the class. In 2010 this visitor was Railfreight Construction-liveried 31271 *Stratford 1840-2001* and this shot sees it arriving at Harmans Cross, bound for Swanage. This loco is currently based on the Churnet Valley Railway. 7 May 2010.

This time we see the loco drifting downhill at Quarr Farm level crossing, just south of Harmans Cross, also heading for Swanage. 9 May 2010.

Right: 31271 *Stratford 1840-2001* is seen arriving at the unmistakable location of Corfe Castle with a Swanage-bound train. Alongside, 47580 *County of Essex* waits to depart for Norden. 8 May 2010.

Below: A year before 31271 visited, the annual gala welcomed 'skinhead' 31108 in immaculate Railfreight livery. This shot sees it departing Norden for Harmans Cross, 'top and tail' with 33103 *Swordfish*, which was resident on the line at the time. The 31's current base is at the Midland Railway Centre, whilst 33103 has moved to pastures new at the Ecclesbourne Valley Railway. 10 May 2009.

This time we see the loco rounding the curve on Corfe Common as it heads for Corfe Castle and Norden with a train from Swanage. 9 May 2009.

Left: Is there a better view than this on a UK heritage line, I wonder? 31108 is captured at Afflington, between Harmans Cross and Corfe Castle, with a Swanage-bound train. 9 May 2009.

Below: The original Railfreight livery really seemed to suit the class; here we see 31108 at Quarr Farm Crossing, just south of Harmans Cross, with a train For Norden. 8 May 2009.

Moving to 2016, it was the turn of 31162 to pay a visit to the diesel gala. Here we see the BR blue loco about to cross Corfe Viaduct with a train from Swanage to Norden. It is virtually impossible to get a shot of a train with a clear road here, especially in the extremely busy spring and summer months! 6 May 2016.

Right: A crew member has the token for the signaller as the loco, with many heads out of windows, approaches Harmans Cross with a train for Swanage. 6 May 2016.

Below: Back again to 2013 when 31466, the sole member of the class to have worked on the main line in EWS livery, was a popular visitor. The loco is seen arriving at Corfe Castle with a Norden-bound train. 10 May 2013.

A powerful shot of 31466 as it approaches Harmans Cross with a Norden to Swanage train. The 'Sussex Scot' headboard refers to an inter-regional train that ran between Brighton and Glasgow/Edinburgh from the mid-1980s until the early 2000s. I am not sure what the significance is with this loco, however; perhaps it actually once hauled one of those trains. 11 May 2013.

Another view of 31466, this time just south of Harmans Cross with a Norden-bound train. I have no idea what the headboard refers to this time, but 'DFDA' appertains to the Dean Forest Diesel Association, who I think still own the loco. At the time of writing, it is on hire to the Severn Valley Railway. 11 May 2013.

Next up we see the loco awaiting departure from Harmans Cross with a train for Norden. This image was taken from the signal box steps with permission. That 'Sussex Scot' headboard has appeared again! 11 May 2013.

This is an unusual pairing of EWS-liveried locos. 31466+37521 *English China Clays* head south round the curve at Afflington, between Corfe Castle and Harmans Cross, with a Norden to Swanage service. 37521 had just been resurrected from the scrapyard, hence the very faded and battered-looking paintwork. Despite its appearance it went on to return to the national network; firstly with Colas Rail for use on test trains, and currently for Locomotive Services Ltd in BR green livery, where it sees occasional use on charter trains. 11 May 2013.

An unusual decision during 2019 was the painting of recently restored 31163 into Derby Research livery under the identity of 97205. The loco never appeared with this number or livery in BR days, but 31298 & 31326 did, as 97203 & 97204 respectively, though both have long since been scrapped. It was very soon after this repaint that this loco appeared at the 2019 Swanage gala; it is seen here at Harmans Cross station with a Norden-bound train. 10 May 2019.

On the section of the Swanage Railway that is not currently in regular use, 97205 is seen crossing Stoborough Heath (near Furzebrook) as it heads towards the end of Swanage Railway jurisdiction at the Frome River Bridges, near the junction with the main line at Worgret. 10 May 2019.

Above: Close to the location in the previous view, this time 97205 is seen approaching a public foot crossing on Stoborough Heath as it heads a train from Swanage to the Frome River Bridges. 11 May 2019.

Right: Here is an almost 'worm's eye view' of 97205 coming around the curve at Afflington and approaching Harmans Cross with a train from Norden to Swanage. 11 May 2019.

The most recent member of the class to visit at the time of writing was BR blue 31128 *Charybdis*, which we saw in the previous chapter of this book being used extensively with Fragonset Railways. It is currently the only example registered for main line use and often sees service on the summer dated runs from Pickering to Whitby. Taking a break from these duties, it is approaching Corfe Castle with a train bound for Norden. 6 May 2022.

Looking in the other direction from the same location as the previous shot, we see 31128 *Charybdis* heading away up the gradient from Corfe Castle with a train for Swanage. 6 May 2022.

Hard to believe this image was taken over 20 years ago. 31108 is seen on the Severn Valley Railway, approaching Bewdley station with a train bound for Kidderminster. 29 September 2000.

Another view of 31108, this time at Kidderminster (SVR) station. The station here was constructed in the late 1800s style of architecture and opened back in 1984, being built on the site of an old goods yard. Over the years it has gradually been improved with various additions. 29 September 2000.

Back in the South West we have an interesting comparison. 31108 is seen at Buckfastleigh on a visit to the South Devon Railway in 2008, alongside the line's resident 33002 *Sea King*. Both locos are in immaculate Railfreight livery. Which one do you prefer? 26 April 2008.

One of the favourite photographic locations along the South Devon Railway is where the line runs close to the picturesque River Dart, locally known as Hood Bridge. 31108 looks superb as it passes beneath, hauling a DMU with a Buckfastleigh to Totnes Littlehempston service. 26 April 2008.

We have now arrived at The East Somerset Railway where in 2003/04 the line held a couple of excellent diesel galas. Prominent at both were Fragonset 31s, which at the time were based at nearby Westbury for working loco-hauled services to Weymouth etc., as seen in the second part of this book. Although this line is quite short, there are a couple of good photographic vantage points. Cranmore station is the operating base, and it is here we see 31128 *Charybdis* arriving from the current westerly limit of the line at Mendip Vale, just under a mile from Shepton Mallet. To the left is 31452 *Minotaur*, which will attach to the other end of the train to form the next departure. 17 April 2004.

This view shows 31468 *Hydra* coming through the deep rock cutting near to Mendip Vale with a train from Cranmore. 5 April 2003.

Mendip Vale is just out of shot above the train in this view as 31468 *Hydra* heads west for Cranmore. 5 April 2003.

Above: During my visit in 2004, some trackside vegetation clearance had taken place around Mendip Vale, opening up this view of 31452 *Minotaur* approaching the small platform here, just out of shot to the left. 17 April 2004.

Left: This is 31452 *Minotaur*, heading up the gradient past the loco shed and works at Cranmore with a train for Mendip Vale. In the far distance behind the train, Cranmore station can just be made out. 17 April 2004.

Looking in the other direction at Merryfield Lane, close to where the previous shot was taken, we see 31128 *Charybdis* + 31452 *Minotaur* approaching with a train for Cranmore. 17 April 2004.

Another view of 31452 *Minotaur* soon after arriving at Cranmore. In more recent years, the station here has received a brand new platform in place of the grassy bank to the left; the original one was removed many years ago. Incidentally, the Mk2 air-conditioned coaches being hauled were a rake used during the week sandwiched between the 31s, whereas the locos and coaches were not normally used on timetabled services at weekends. 17 April 2004.

31128 *Charybdis* is seen pulling away from Cranmore with a service for Mendip Vale. Although the signal box has remained from days gone by, it does not operate any signals or points at present. Another visiting loco, 37674 *Saint Blaise Church 1445-1995*, can be seen to the right. 17 April 2004.

To take our leave of the East Somerset Railway, we see 31452 *Minotaur* + 31128 *Charybdis* side by side at Cranmore station. 17 April 2004.

For the conclusion of this section, we move east again to the Mid-Hants Railway, another line that has seen plenty of Class 31 activity during the well-known 'Trainspotters' Ball' diesel galas. At a time when lineside photographic passes were issued by this line for an annual cost, 31162, with an Alton to Alresford train, is passing a superb patch of cowslips on the approaches to Ropley. 27 April 2002.

Here we see 31162 piloting 50031 *Hood* as they ascend the gradient away from Ropley towards Medstead & Four Marks with an Alton-bound service. 27 April 2002.

This time 31162 is pulling into Medstead & Four Marks with another Alton-bound train. 27 April 2002.

31162 is ticking over patiently as it waits at Medstead & Four Marks to cross a southbound train heading for Alresford. 27 April 2002.

Some years before its visit to the Swanage Railway that we saw earlier, 31271 was a guest at the Mid-Hants during 2003. Unfortunately, my visit here was again dogged by rain! Almost appearing to be sheltering from this precipitation, the loco is seen beneath the canopy at Alresford. 16 May 2003.

Left: Powering away from Ropley, 31271 is coming up the gradient as it heads toward Medstead & Four Marks and, ultimately, Alton. 17 May 2003.

Below: Due to the gradient at this location, this is a very popular part of the line with photographers. This shot sees Alton-bound 31271 making another assault of it at just about the same spot as the previous image, but from a much wider perspective. 17 May 2003.

On Ropley station there are a couple of lovely shrubs kept in tip-top condition by someone with an obvious interest in topiary! 31271 has now arrived with an Alresford to Alton train but it seems that, apart from a person at the other end of the platform and the station porter keeping dry under the canopy, I was the only other person to brave the conditions! 16 May 2003.

Right: Another of those well-trimmed shrubs is seen here as 31271 comes past Ropley signal box with an Alton to Alresford train. The locomotive workshops can be seen behind the box. 16 May 2003.

Below: The Fragonset locos used to get everywhere back then! 31128 *Charybdis* is seen again, this time approaching Ropley with an Alton to Alresford train. 14 May 2005.

Framed by semaphore signals, 31128 *Charybdis* is seen exiting the siding at Alresford to head the next train to Alton. 14 May 2005.

Our last shot in this section sees another favourite again as 31108 departs from Ropley with an Alton to Alresford train. 14 May 2005.

Chapter 4

Open Days and Events

For the last section of this book, we see a few locos that have featured at various open days and events.

Above: This is 31403, stabled at Old Oak Common depot during one of the many open days that have been held here in the past. This loco was scrapped in 2003. 15 September 1985.

Right: Fragonset 31601 *Bletchley Park – Station X* on view at the Crewe open day. Once again, I have no idea what that headboard refers to. 20 May 2001.

Here we see 31158 inside the shed at the popular Plymouth Laira open day. Unfortunately, the loco was scrapped in 2003. 7 September 1985.

Before its later exploits with Network Rail that we saw earlier in this book, this is 31105 *Bescot TMD – Bescot & Saltley Quality Assured* on display at the superb Exeter Rail Fair that was held in Riverside Yard. 2 May 1994.

Open Days and Events

Another member of the class on view at the Exeter Rail Fair was a smart-looking InterCity 'Mainline' liveried 31422. Rather surprisingly, this loco was not scrapped until 2014. 2 May 1994.

Well, what can you say about this one! Unique Infrastructure-liveried 31116 *RAIL – Celebrity* shows off its unusual colours at the Exeter Rail Fair. This bright livery was actually an experiment to assess a suitable colour scheme for engineers' locos allocated to the South East area in 1993, prior to privatisation. Eventually, the 'aircraft blue' of Mainline Freight superseded it before any more locos were painted. Class 47 No 47803 did carry a similar livery at one point, gaining it the nickname 'The Yellow Peril'. The 31 was not actually scrapped until 2003, the Class 47 following during 2007. 2 May 1994.

Another very popular event in the late 1980s was the Basingstoke Rail Fair, held in the down yard sidings (now mostly built on). No special example this time, just 31286, which was a recent recipient of the revised 'red stripe' Railfreight livery and looking very tidy. 26 September 1987.

Our friend 31108 again, this time looking as immaculate as ever at the Old Oak Common open day. 5 August 2000.

Another 'skinhead', 31110 *Traction Magazine* became something of a 'celebrity' following a repaint into original BR green livery. It is perhaps surprising that the loco was scrapped in 2007 and did not enter preservation. 5 August 2000.

Not exactly on display, Regional Railways-liveried 31465 is viewed during the open day at Old Oak Common amongst the stored locos. In the mid-1990s, just prior to privatisation, BR operated various loco-hauled passenger trains under the Regional Railways identity. The half a dozen or so Class 31s painted in this livery were mainly restricted to the North of England and North Wales areas. Of course, it was far from curtains for this particular loco, as it went on to have a lengthy career on the main line with Network Rail, and has recently entered preservation. 5 August 2000.

The final image in this book depicts the first loco built! This is 31018 (the original D5500) on display at its permanent home in the National Railway Museum at York. This is the only Class 31/0 that I have seen; in the late 1970s I was still but a teenager with only a bicycle for transport, and the nearest point I stood a chance of seeing one was many miles from my home area. The odds of one turning up in deepest Dorset in those days was just about nil, even on a charter! 25 February 2022.

Other books you might like:

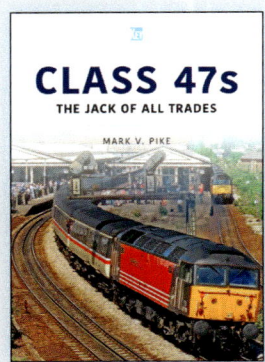
Britain's Railways Series, Vol. 45

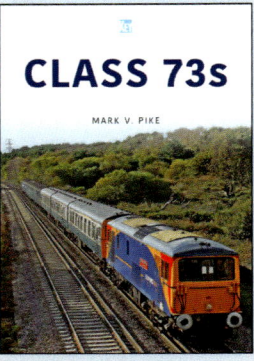
Britain's Railways Series, Vol. 41

Britain's Railways Series, Vol. 39

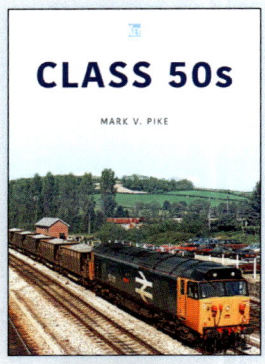
Britain's Railways Series, Vol. 36

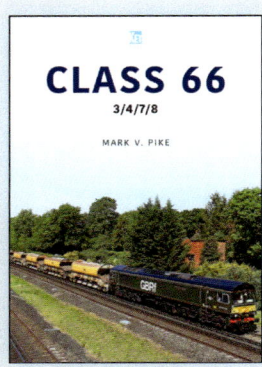
Britain's Railways Series, Vol. 35

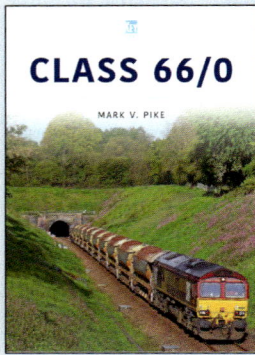
Britain's Railways Series, Vol. 32

For our full range of titles please visit:
shop.keypublishing.com/books

VIP Book Club

Sign up today and receive
TWO FREE E-BOOKS

Be the first to find out about our forthcoming book releases and receive exclusive offers.

Register now at keypublishing.com/vip-book-club

Our VIP Book Club is a 100% spam-free zone, and we will never share your email with anyone else. You can read our full privacy policy at: privacy.keypublishing.com